PSYCHOPATH PSYCHOLOGY

LETS UNDERSTAND WHAT IS INSIDE OF PSYCHOPATHIC MIND

SHREYASH MASKARE

Made with ♥ on the Notion Press Platform
www.notionpress.com

Contents

Important

Hi, as you are beginning this journey, I want you to commit to complete it upto End.

And most importantly don't skip the last chapter (chapter no. 4)

Now lets start this journey together...

...

We all have wear the glasses of illusion according to our thoughts and beliefs.

But to see the real world we have to remove them.

If tou think you are big,
you become small.
If you know you are nothing,
you become unlimited.
And that's the beauty of being a human being.
-Sadhguru

CHAPTER ONE

Evil within Smile

What does evil look like?

Could you spot it, If it walked into the room?

Serial killers look just like you and me,

The darkness they share isn't written all over their faces

It's in their mind.

-Criminal mind cost

Wanna hear a story? Come on, let's hear one.

It was the year 2007, In the District Begusarai in Bihar, India, there's a small village named 'Mushahari', It was a normal day in the village. Until Chunchun Devi left her 6 - month old daughter Khushboo in care at local primary school like everyday and left for work. But when she returned, her daughter Khushboo was missing. As usual like any mother Chunchun Devi got worried. She's a mother, so she would be concerned, right? Now when such a small daughter gets lost, somewhere you can understand how a mother must be feeling. She becomes worried and becomes crazy. She starts asking everyone, 'Have you seen my daughter? But no one has a clue about it.

Later after a while one of the member of Sada family (neighbors of Chunchun Devi)

Came to her and told her that maybe they knew where her daughter could be. They went to the Bhagwannagar police station and reported the case. And as this was a case of a small child, Police start taking action on it immediately. During the time of investigation, Police realize that similar incidents have happened before. Not once, but twice. That means, two girls are already missing from the village. When more interrogation is done, then they get to know that both these girls were members of the Sada family. Slowly the villagers get to know that not only 1 but 3 girls are missing from the village. And the whole village falls into chaos. Now, the member of the Sada family who is helping the police, takes them to a playground. where the police meet the 8-year-old kid Amarjeet Sada for the first time. You must be thinking what does this 8 year old kid will know about this, But here where the actual story begins. They ask Amarjeet if he has seen Khushboo? But the child doesn't say anything, and just smiles. Now for some reason, the police think that the child knows something. Maybe he has seen someone who kidnapped Khushboo? Because of this, they took Amarjeet to the police station.

Now, In normal circumstances any other kid will get scared or will behave nervously, But Amarjeet's behavior in the police station is very different. Amarjeet isn't scared. In fact, he was smiling. He was observing things. And if any police officer asks something to him then he says, 'First, give me a biscuit, then I'll talk.' Finally, when a police officer gives him a pack of biscuits. Amarjeet becomes happy and says, 'Yes, I know where Khushboo is.' He says that Khushboo is dead now and he knows this because he has killed Khushboo.

That sounds unbelievable right? A 8 year old kid is confessing that he has killed a 6 month old child. But as the conversations continue things start getting worse. After listening to all of this. It becomes important for the police to know how Amarjeet does this. To this when they asked him, Amarjeet says that he was in school when he saw Khushboo. She was alone. So, Amarjeet took her from there. After taking her among the trees, he tried to strangle her neck. But he says that when he was strangling her neck, he wasn't having fun, he didn't get the satisfaction. He wanted to see that pain, the fear, the compulsion in Khushboo's eyes, but he didn't see it. Which is why he leaves her, takes a brick and hits her until she isn't dead.

After listening to this, the police were shocked! Amarjeet's case was very complicated and terrifying . He was born in 1998 and his family was very poor. His dad was a wage worker, and his mom was a housewife. Because of not having money, this family thought that they'll move to Mushahari village. At that time, Amarjeet was 6 years old. Amarjeet was a disturbed child. There was always a violent, murderous streak within him. He used to argue with people, trouble them, fight with them. And its frequency was growing every day. Not only villagers but even his family knew about Amarjeet's this type of behavior. In fact, his family has even experienced his violent streak. The two girls who had gone missing from this family, Amarjeet had murdered both of them. Out of them, one was Amarjeet's cousin's sister who was 6 years old and the other one was Amarjeet's sibling who was 6 months old at that time. But the most painful and horrible thing was, Amarjeet killed both of his sisters the same cruel way he murdered Khushboo. And the most unfortunate thing was Amarjeet's family knew this. They knew that Amarjeet was behind all this. But due to some reason, they decided that they'll hide this from everyone. And that was their biggest mistake. Because in 2008, after killing Khushboo, Amarjeet became India's Youngest Serial Killer in History.

That seems to be an unbelievable story right? But the painful truth is this is an actual incident. But what do you think, why would a 8 year old kid will perform such a horrible crime? Amarjeet is not a professional criminal right? Neither he has murdered them for any purposeful reason like for getting money or revenge like most of the crimes were done. And the horrible part is he not only killed them but killed them brutally. What makes this incident makes us question is whether there is a difference between a criminal and a psychopath. And Is Amarjeet was a psychopath.

After Amarjeet's confession, many psychologists did medical investigations on this, because it was necessary to know why that kid did it. There was no one from his family from a criminal background, Neither there was any TV or radio in his house through which he could know about crime. After that because Amarjeet was an 8-year-old kid, as per the Indian Law, the Indian Constitution, if any person is below 18, then he can't be put in jail. Until he turned 18, he was in a child care home. And just as he turned 18, He was released.

But again we came to the same questions that How and Why someone will do that. And not only about this case there are several cases we hear everyday, especially on news channels where they show what's going on in the country later and show these types of cases first.

And it's get hard for us to understand these types of people, Because Psychology is a field of science But, however, is not a science. It's a subject area. And you can either study it scientifically or non-scientifically. It can be a debatable topic But as we see Science tends to go through these shifts therefore psychology is not a science as it has no agreed paradigm. Everyone's thought process is different, everyone's perspective of seeing a situation is different, because every brain works differently. So, does that mean this is all related to the brain?

So, without making it complicated the simple answer would be "Yes", It is all about the brain. But it is not as simple as it sounds. Because a question arises that How? What makes a person a psychopath, how their brain becomes so emotionless that they do not even feel guilt while performing such a horrible act, and most importantly "Why we are not like them" . But there is also a question arise that, why its gets important for us to understand it, Its gets because, for understanding them we need to understand the human brain, And understanding the brain can lead us to understanding of ourselves. And it also gets important because many times we face situations where we discover a negative side of ourselves where we think differently and act differently.

Once Psychologist professor of University of Texas at Austin,

David Buss has conducted a survey of 5000 students, where he discovered that approx

91% of mens and 76% of females sometime or another have thought of the idea of killing someone. And in another survey he discovered that in 2018 a average men has fantasize 10 times of murdering someone and 3 times by womens. It sounds shocking right? Well not, Now, That sounds weird but to understand this, we need to understand the evolution of the brain Because..........

Everything that irritates us about others, can lead us to an Understanding of ourselves.

-Carl Jung

So, Let's move to next chapter ...

CHAPTER TWO

UNDERSTANDING THE HUMAN BRAIN

The Human brain , then, is the most complicated organization of matter that we know.

-Issac Asimov

We all know that we are not alone on this planet. If we believe the statistics, then there are millions of different species on the whole earth. But whenever we will talk about the most intelligent one, humans will raise their hand first. Which is true, homo sapiens are the most intelligent species on earth. But are we always like that? Are we the most intelligent from the beginning? In our early times most probably 10,000 B.C. the time which was also known as stone age, we also used to live in caves and jungles like other animals. People used to hunt for their survival.

So, basically if we compare an early age man with a modern age man we will find out the huge differences. So what's the reason behind this development? The reason was the process of development which is known as Evolution. And specifically we can say Evolution of Human brain.

We are aware of this fact. Maybe some can debate on this but after all we can't deny the fact that we are the result of Evolution . But have we achieved the final level of evolution? Are Homo sapiens are the highest level of evolution? The simple answer is "No".

If we go through the scientific definition of evolution. "Evolution is change in the heritable characteristics of biological populations over successive generations. "

Evolution means the creation continues, which means we are just a new level, but the cycle will go further away. Evolution does not means progress, evolution just ensures change, so that organisms can survive in current circumstances. Therefore homo sapiens are not the ultimate form of humans. But still there is something that makes us different. Biologically all the creatures may stand together but culturally we are very different. And it's not hard to see the difference, other animals still live in forests but we have left the forests long ago. Other animals still have to struggle and fight for food, on the other hand humans don't have to face such type of scenario until they have money. And if we compared the lifestyle as compared to any other creatures. We live in a very complex cultural setting. Because we have gone forward with the basic requirement of survival. We don't usually think about the danger and survival. Do you remember the last time you were really hungry, not talking about normal hunger but real hunger means not having eaten for days. Normally We get food from time to time. Today, after completing our meal we do different types of activities like painting, learning something new, reading books and news, listening to music, working on our goals and now we are planning to move the humans to another planet. Basically we live with purpose. So, how we get able to do such tasks, we can do this because of our brain. Our brain gives us capability to think out of the box, it gives us power to turn a dream into reality. And the interesting thing is it's not about the intelligence of the human brain, nor about the size. Because intelligence is something which is hard to measure and there are so many intelligent organisms in the ecosystem who can use tools like us, they also live in community, they also have complexity in their social life, some animals also perform death rituals, elephants are the example. And if it is about the size of the brain then there are so many animals who have bigger brains than humans, For example Elephants have bigger brains than humans, eventually 3 times bigger and if it is matter of brain the blue have the biggest brain of approx 9 kg which is so much as large compared to humans. And on the other hand Human brain is only of 1.2kg to 1.4kg.

So, the power of the brain depends on the number of neurons our brain has.

And specifically the number of neurons in our cerebral cortex or neocortex have (Both are the same).

Brain evolution

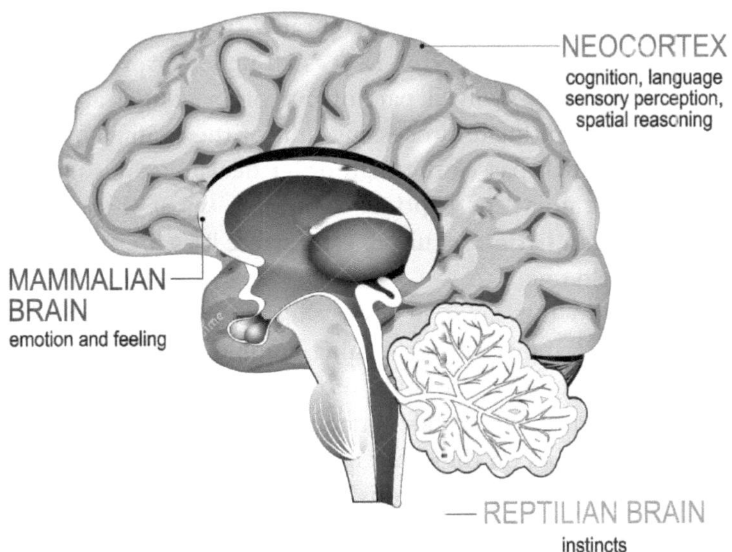

So, first let's talk about what neurons are. Neurons are the brain cells. As we know for the proper working of the body different organs work together in their ways and all of these organs are made up of cells. And the cells of every organ are specialized in their own way like muscle cell, stem cell, nerve cell, skin cell. That's why we are multicellular organisms. Actually there are two forms of life: single cellular and multicellular, which means collection of cells. When we will understand it deeply we will realize that, we are nothing but the collection of cells or our body is nothing but collection of cells and we are just a consciousness which is formed from supreme consciousness. But that's a different topic.

And neurons do not limit itself to only upto the brain, Neurons can be found everywhere in the body. We can see neurons as an information processing unit. Because it creates a complex circuit with other neurons and communicates with it.

So with the size of the brain the most important thing is how many neurons are there in our cerebral cortex. Now, if you don't know what the cerebral cortex is. It is an upper layer of the brain and it is a recently evolved part of our brain comparatively. We can say it is the ultimate processing unit of the brain. This is part of the brain which passes the high order decisions like sensation, reasoning, memory, perception. Normally what happens, for making an organ better, nature doesn't make it again. Instead they improve the old one.

In our brain this layer of cortex has been developed, which gives us the capability of performing complex tasks. So, neurons are the reasons behind the main difference between humans and any other creatures. If we take one example Elephants brain have 5.6 billions neurons on the other hand humans brain have total 86 billions neurons, where 16 billions are in cerebral cortex and others in remaining part of brain.

AnimalsNo. of neurons

Humans 86 billions

Elephants 5.6 billions

Mouse 30 millions

Chimpanzee 3.6 billions

Ape 9 billions

So, because of those densely packed neurons are the reason behind why we are better at working comparatively. This is the reason, we can think so complexly, we can do future planning. But, But, But, there are some exceptions related to this study.

Actually these study was conducted by Brazilian neuroscientist

"Suzana herculano-houzel" and if you wanna know more about these study, you can find these on the internet.

But now at least we are as much aware with the working of the brain that now we can move on towards our next chapter. Because without understanding brain we can't even understand ourselves, so how can we understand others?

Now, let us move towards our main chapter Because...

The more you know about something, the better you can handle it. The more you know about Yourself, the better you can handle Yourself. This is called self-realization.

-Sadhguru

Before starting this chapter, Come on, let's hear a one short story. Once there was a boy "Tariku". One day while returning from school he saw a lot of carrots in the nearby garden, so without knowing the owner of the garden he entered there and took some carrots home. He went home and said to his mother, "Mom, I have bought some carrots, prepare me a delicious soup today with these carrots". His mother asked, "From where do you get these carrots ?". He replied, "These are from the nearby garden". She knew that Tariku had taken these without the permission of the owner. But his mother didn't pay attention to it but rather prepared him a delicious soup. Balu was happy as he wasn't punished for his mistakes. Because she was already in tension because of her abusive husband who used to blame her for every problem in his life. After that Tariku continued stealing things but as time went on, his desires started increasing. So he started to steal big things from others. But this time he was caught and the police took him to the police station. After hearing news about her son His mother rushed to the police station. After seeing her son's situation, She started to cry. At that time Tariku said to her, "There is no need to cry now. You encouraged my mistakes during my childhood days, that's why I am in this situation now".

If you have punished me on that day, "I might be a good person at present". Now leave this place. And suddenly her tears turned into anger and she shouted at him and said "Why are you blaming me, If you know what is wrong and what is right then why you chose this path" And she leaves.

Now tell me, After listening to this story what do you think whose mistake was this. And the situation is you have to choose any one.

See it is easy to choose between good or bad or right or wrong. But in some cases there might be a situation where maybe both are wrong or maybe both are right in their own way.

Now it's all up to you and your perspective on how to see this situation.

Now leave it and let us move on to our chapter.....

CHAPTER THREE

UNDERSTANDING THE PSYCHOPATHY

we need to get that arousal in a good way. We don't like feeling it when we do something wrong. But They don't feel it.

It is believed that psychopaths are born with a genetic predisposition., whether it's due to a gene being passed on or to a brain abnormality, while sociopaths are created from unstable, often abusive early childhoods.

Psychopaths and sociopaths share a number of characteristics, including a lack of remorse or empathy for others, a lack of guilt or ability to take responsibility for their actions, a disregard for laws or social conventions, and an inclination to violence. A core feature of both is a deceitful and manipulative nature.

Sociopaths are normally less emotionally stable and highly impulsive-their behavior tends to be more erratic than psychopaths. When committing crimes-either violent or non-violent-sociopaths will act more on compulsion. And they will lack patience, giving in much more easily to impulsiveness and lacking detailed planning.

Psychopaths, on the other hand, will plan their crimes down to the smallest detail, taking calculated risks to avoid detection. The smart ones will leave few clues that may lead to being caught. Psychopaths don't get carried away in the moment and make fewer mistakes as a result.

Both act on a continuum of behaviors, and many psychologists still debate whether the two should be differentiated at all. But for those who do differentiate between the two, one thing is largely agreed upon: psychiatrists use the term psychopathy to illustrate that the cause of the antisocial personality disorder is hereditary.

Sociopathy describes behaviors that are the result of a brain injury, or abuse and/or neglect in childhood.

Psychopaths are born and sociopaths are made. In essence, their difference reflects the nature versus nurture debate. There's a particularly interesting link between serial killers and psychopaths or sociopaths-although, of course, not all psychopaths and sociopaths become serial killers. And not all serial killers are psychopaths or sociopaths.

Normal vs Abnormal behavior

See, our belief, mutual understanding, common interests.

These are the things that bind us together in society.

Even after being complete strangers to each other, We transact with one another without hesitation. We transact with money, things, etc.

We believe that the other party will not cheat. And most of the time they don't.

It's not always that people do not want to cheat.

But to live in a society or a big community of people means that you have to have control over your selfish tendencies. Be it a human society or even an animal herd of any scale, There are rules that the individuals of the society obey.

You can't just have it all for yourself.

It is also called **Dharma in Hinduism** - ***The balance between your free will and your social responsibility.***

You also need to consider people who are around you.

You cannot satisfy your desires by taking advantage of or abusing people. That is not moral.

Your biological inclinations need to be managed. You need to act more politely around other people. We all agree that each person in this room is an original person with unique human rights. You cannot and will not be harmed by anyone.

And those who will not follow it will get punished.

This is how a huge, huge community of people goes about its daily business. Together, we adjust. We restrain our savage, wild tendencies.

Additionally, these moral standards are taught to us as we develop. ,but still, we all are selfish to some degree. We all are more or less selfish with one or the other aspect of our life.

But there are some people whose personality is encompassed by selfishness.

In fact, they are the embodiment of selfishness and anti-sociality.

And we are talking exactly about these types of people. They are experts in manipulating and exploiting people. They don't care about your feelings, nor do they ever get emotional themselves. They are selfish because they only acknowledge their own existence. They don't even consider others as individuals. They don't have any ethical boundaries. They throw humility out of the window. They have no remorse, and also they are emotionally shallow. Guilt and remorse do not exist in their vocabulary.

And with these, if there are violent tendencies, then it's even worse.

They are the real threat to social structure and social hierarchy.

Narcissism

Narcissism is a type of personality behavior. Many people think that narcissists are psychopaths because Narcissistic personality disorder — one of several types of personality disorders — is a mental condition in which people have an inflated sense of their own importance, a deep need for excessive attention and admiration, troubled relationships, and a lack of empathy for others. But behind this mask of extreme confidence lies a fragile self-esteem that's vulnerable to the slightest criticism.

A narcissistic personality disorder causes problems in many areas of life, such as relationships, work, school or financial affairs. People with narcissistic personality disorder may be generally unhappy and disappointed when they're not given the special favors or admiration they believe they deserve. Narcissist is somebody who lacks empathy, is entitled, is constantly seeking validation, and is arrogant. It's a disorder of self-esteem and they have trouble regulating their self-esteem. But when a narcissist does a bad thing, They feel a fair amount of guilt and shame. More shame than guilt, because they're concerned about how other people view them. Shame is a public emotion. So they don't like being viewed negatively in the public eye or by other people– that's where the shame comes from. But they'll feel a little bad. Like if they cheat on their wife, They might feel bad and guilty. But a psychopath's a different animal. They're all of those things except: no guilt/ no shame. They don't feel remorse when they do something bad. For explaining narcissist personality we can say extreme egoist personality.

So, here's the key rule to remember: "Every psychopath is narcissistic, but not every narcissist is psychopathic."

Psychopaths are born, and sociopaths are made.

So, we have discussed that, Psychopaths are born. their belief is that. This might be genetic. In fact psychopaths often have fathers who have lots of antisocial tendencies.

Now how much of it is learned, How much of it is genetic It's a little bit harder to figure out.

If you remember the story of Amarjeet, which we have discussed in the first part, that 8 year old boy who has killed 3 kids is a true example of a psychopath. As we have analyzed his behavior, We can understand psychopathic mind. See when we diagnose Antisocial Personality Disorder,

which is sort of our diagnostic equivalent to being a psychopath. In order to get that diagnosis

They may shown a pattern prior to the age of 15 of things like:

Truancy, violence towards other kids, stealing, skipping school, not felt bad about it torturing animals, setting fires.

They just do it. They don't care and these can be seen at an early age . So it's a long-standing pattern

That's what makes us call them a psychopath or having antisocial personality.

Now, if we wanna take example of sociopath we can say:

"Hey you remember that kid he was actually a great kid until he got to high school and then it seems like he got in with the wrong kid". That feels more like a sociopath.

But it said that sociopaths are actually more dangerous for society because they have learned this behavior because of society. Sociopathy, they look a lot like psychopaths.

The difference is they were made.

So this...some examples here...the kid who grows up in a really, really rough neighborhood and learns criminality to get by

or learns to be a bully or like you know gets involved with sort of like

the wrong kids and uses a lot of muscle, Because that's survivalism,

But they...it's not necessarily always comfortable for them. They just learn it.

It's the person who grows up with a father who teaches them the business and teaches them how to break the rules.

But Now, why rather than all why only some peoples do such horrible crimes:

According to studies when a person does not control his emotions mostly in anger he commits a crime. One study has tell four main reason behind of becoming a serial killer where

36% of peoples are victims of physical abuse in childhood

26% of peoples are victims of sexual abuse

18% of peoples of Neglect means state of not getting food, shelter, and any emotional care

And remaining were victims of psychological abuse.

Overall maximum serial killers are victims of child abuse. Which has left a very dangerous and negative impact on them.

Some of the solutions for dealing with psychopathy:

The most successful approaches to treating psychopathy are multimodal. This means they include multiple approaches at once, including psychotherapy, behavioral skills training, and recognition of the important roles of family, school, peers, and the community. They may also incorporate medication.

If someone sees psychopathy in a child they can deal with it by Responsive parenting behaviors which includes, for example, expressing concern through your face and voice, asking questions, or offering a hug if your child is upset. Some research suggests that children with psychopathy are less sensitive than other children to positive social and emotional cues.

But if home-based treatment methods have not been successful. Medications are appropriate for some children, adolescents and adults in combination with other forms of therapy. Medication should not be a first-line treatment.

Research has shown that taking some food items on a diet eventually can make someone less aggressive. According to a study, if we give omega 3 fatty acid in the diet of prisoners it can make them 40% less violent in some months.

Along with some change in diet, proper therapy can be very helpful for changing one's behavior.

But the thing is psychopaths never go to therapy unless it's a court order, Because they don't find it useless for them. So, yes we can say that "The failure of parenting and social environment leads to psychopathy". That's why we need to save the beauty of childhood, In this competition of winning in this so-called modern society we need to make sure that love, humbleness, kindness, care wins over ego, anger and comparison.

We need to make sure that positive emotions wins over negativity.

But there is more to the story....Therefore let's move towards the finale and most beautiful chapter of our journey......

CHAPTER FOUR

WHY YOU ARE NOT A PSYCHOPATH

Nowadays, every person have his own beliefs, values, ideology.

And the thing is we are one, who have developed those ideologies. And as compared to others no other creatures are able to do this. That's why when a person is a kid he or she have cuteness, innocence, simplicity but among these one thing they have is countless possibility of what they can be in future.

And as much as it makes me feel excited it also freaks me out. Because obviously the future of the world and mankind is in the hands of these little kids. They can be be the reason for chaos or the reason for peace.

Because we are the ones who maintain the eternal balance of chaos and order, right and wrong, good and evil and war and peace in this world. And it's all matter on the decision of that person. That, what we choose to be. And any person takes those decisions on the basis of their past events and trauma. Or we can say because of their suffering.

See, **Life is a suffering,** and it's an eternal truth, no one can deny. And as per our modern society, if you wanna be successful in life you have to struggle a lot.

And the main reason behind our suffering, which I think, is we humans are insanely weak in terms of emotions and physique. Anything can break us whether mentally or physically.

Eventually almost every person is surrounded by lots of problems. Where some are in their control, some are very serious, and some problems are not really a problem but we think it is.

And there are very few people who at any given time are not struggling with at least one serious problem, especially when we include their family in the equation.

But after all this the biggest cruise our beautiful nature has given us is the punishment of death.

Even if you are extremely attractive or have a pleasant face, with time it all fades away.

We are all allegedly born with a death sentence. Even if we don't commit anything wrong, still one day we have to pass away. And one day our loved one's will also leave us.

What can be a bigger injustice than this in our life? Therefore people try to get over suffering. The suffering of losing our loved one's, the suffering of losing ourselves, the suffering of emotions. And getting over suffering, our religion gives us hope and tells us the way to get over it.

Hinduism teaches us to achieve **"moksha"** which means to get release from the cycle of rebirth. In Buddhism, the meaning of Nirvana is to get over suffering.

But sometimes some people get unable to control the spark of their emotions and after getting completely broken in their life, after being fully crushed by life. They reached to one of these two conclusions -

1)It is better not to be at all.

and **2), perhaps it would be even better if there is no being at all.**

For any human being, these two are very dangerous conclusions of life. People who reach the first conclusion are flirting with suicide.. They rely on dying themselves to end their pain.

Cesare Pavese (Italian novelist) has said ***"Nobody lacks a good reason for suicide."***

No one ever lacks a good reason for suicide.

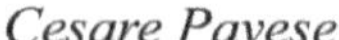
Cesare Pavese

And those who reach the second conclusion are even more dangerous.

Far more horrific. One who is filled with feelings of revenge.

Someone who actually commits something truly monsters acts.

Everyone is their enemy. And they want to kill everyone.

They enjoy the destruction of everything. These are the people who are completely feeling less. The one who is unable to feel emotions.

These are the people who become Murders, rapists, serial-killers, dictators, cannibalists, terrorists and so on...

and in other words...psychopaths.

They are filled with an ocean of negative and hateful emotions. In fact, in some cases, after doing there horrific crimes, they kill themselves only to show their hatred for life,

to demonstrate the purity of their commitment towards their distracted mindset.

They are like living zombies, a pure face of chaos.

And as per the situations of mankind I believe that we all have our reasons to destroy the world and we are capable of it.

We all have a monster buried up inside us. As there is a saying-

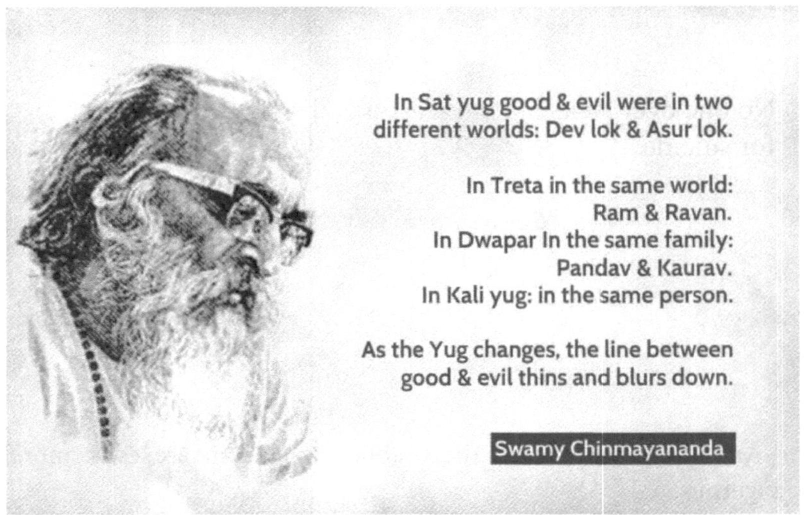

In sat yug the good and evil were in two different worlds.In treta the good and evil were in the same world.In Dwapar the good and evil were in the same family.But Now, In kali yug good and evil lives in a same person.

But then our main question arises that why we are different from them then emerges.

Why didn't we let the psychological and physical traumas in our lives emerge as something terrible? Why do we still suffer from pain in life?

And there are two reasons for this too.

First, suffering makes us strong. You will not deny the fact that whatever problems we have faced after overcoming them we feel more powerful and stronger to live the life ahead. Because as human beings we learn and we adapt.

As Charles Dickens had said-

Suffering has been stronger than all other teaching,

And has taught me to understand what your heart used to be, I have been bent and broken, but I hope- into a better shape.

- Charles Dickens

And the second reason, which is the most important too

is that there is always a meaning to our suffering.

Somehow, our suffering is not just suffering when we find meaning in it.

Like Friedrich Nietzsche had said-

To live is to suffer,

To survive is to find some meaning in the suffering.

Therefore, Even under the worst circumstances, if you keep in mind the person who needs your love the most, you will find the strength to endure it.

If you sincerely believe in your work, you would continue to do it even if no one valued it.

And after losing all sense of meaning in life, people begin displaying psychopathic tendencies. Therefore someone has said, that more than finding pleasure and power in life, We need to find meaning in our lives.

And Because of all this understanding I remembered the one conversation between

Shri Krishna And Karna, In mahabharata there was moment when Karna and Shri Krishna had this conversation Where they talk about the injustice of life:

Where Karna asked Shri Krishna that,

Karna: "My mother left me the moment I was born. Is it my fault I was born an illegitimate child?

I did not get the education from Dhronacharya because I was considered a non-Kshatriya.

Parshuram ji taught me right but cursed that at the time when I would need that education the most, I would forget it. Because according to him I was a Kshatriya.

A cow was accidentally hit by my arrow and its owner cursed me for no fault of mine.

I was disgraced in Draupadi's swayamvar.

Even Kunti Mata finally told me the truth only to save her other sons.

Whatever I received was through Duryodhana's charity. So how am I wrong in taking his side?"

Lord Krishna listens to him patiently and replies:

"Karna, I was born in a jail. Death was waiting for me even before my birth. The night I was born I was separated from my birth parents.

From childhood, you grew up hearing the noise of swords, chariots, horses, bow, and arrows. I got only the cow herd's shed, dung, and multiple attempts on my life even before I could walk! No army, no education.

I could hear people saying I am the reason for all their problems.

When all of you were being appreciated for your valor by your teachers I had not even received any education. I joined gurukula of Rishi Sandipani only at the age of 16.

You are married to a girl of your choice. I didn't get the girl I loved & rather ended up marrying those who wanted me or the ones I rescued from demons.

I had to move my whole community from the banks of Yamuna to a far off Sea shore to save them from Jarasandh. I was called a coward for running away.

If Duryodhana wins the war you will get a lot of credit. What do I get if Yudhishthir wins the war? Only the blame for the war and all related problems...

Remember one thing, Karna. Everybody has challenges in life.

LIFE IS NOT FAIR ON ANYBODY

Duryodhana also has a lot of unfairness in life and so has Yudhishthir.

But what is Right (Dharma) is known to your mind (conscience). No matter how much unfairness we got, how many times we were disgraced, how many times we were denied what was due to us, what is important is how you REACTED at that time.

Stop whining Karna. Life's unfairness does not give you license to walk the wrong path.

Always remember, Life may be tough at a point, but Destiny is not created by the shoes we wear but by the STEPS we take"

This conversation between Karna and Krishna carries a valuable life lesson which is eternally relevant. Most of us justify what we do (usually wrongful acts) by accounting the unjust happenings in our lives. We sulk in self-pity and blame everyone for the hardships we had to go through. We validate our actions by the sufferings we had to face.

It is important to understand that even though the circumstances we face are defined by our Karma, how we choose to react to those circumstances defines our destiny!

While Karna and Krishna both faced similar 'únjust' situations since birth, one grew up to be insecure, jealous and bitter while the latter matured into a secure, wise and empathetic individual. This is the difference between ignorance and awareness.

Take a few moments and peep inside yourself today.

And see, Who lives there? Krishna or Karna?..........

...

Breathing exercise for anger management:

One easy way to calm your body and reduce your anger is to slow and deepen your breathing. Try breathing slowly into your nose and out your mouth. Breathe deeply from your belly rather than your chest. Repeat breaths as necessary.

....

"The most beautiful moments in life are moments when you are expressing your joy, not when you are seeking it."

~ Sadhguru

Thank You...

If you have come upto this page, I really like to thank you for joining me with this journey.

And wants to congratulate you for completing this journey...

And if you want to connect with me you can find me on Instagram.

Hope we will come up with new journey on new topic soon,

Until then, Have a good time...

9 798888 833421

Printed by Libri Plureos GmbH in Hamburg,
Germany